A Comprehensive Method Book for Year One and Beyond

HABITS OF A SUCCESSFUL BEGINNER BAND MUSICIAN

BARITONE SAXOPHONE

SCOTT RUSH
JEFF SCOTT

KEVIN BOYLE
Percussion

EDITED BY
MARGUERITE WILDER

To access *www.habitsuniversal.com*, see the inside front cover for the Student Activation Code.

GIA Publications, Inc.
Your sound. Inspired.

Other Books in the "Habits" series

Habits of a Successful Beginner Band Musician – Baritone Saxophone Edition
Scott Rush • Jeff Scott

G-10168
ISBN: 978-1-62277-477-7

7404 S. Mason Avenue, Chicago, IL 60638
www.giamusic.com

Welcome to the *Habits of a Successful Beginner Band Musician* Series! This beginner method book was written to help you establish an effective daily routine that will build your skills as a musician and introduce you to some of the world's greatest music. As you progress, we hope to inspire you to acquire a love for music and making music. *Habits of a Successful Beginner Band Musician* is the journey from being a first-year music student to blossoming into a passionate artist. This daily routine of technique and skill joined together with musicianship and artistry ultimately leads to great music making. Congratulations on your decision to join band ... now let the music begin!

TIPS FOR HOW TO PRACTICE

Practice your instrument every day!

- Before playing, listen to two minutes of a recording of your favorite artist or go to *Habits Online Universal* and listen to your coach. Try to imitate his or her sound.
- Pick a set time each day to practice.
- Have a set, quiet place to practice.
- Use a straight back chair and a music stand, using good posture.
- Use a metronome and tuner and work on Timing, Tuning, Tone, and Technique.
- Begin the practice session with some stretching and any breathing exercises you've learned in class.
- Play the first notes focusing on great tone quality; First, make a great sound on your MOUTHPIECE AND NECK sounding a concert E; then, make great sounds on the full instrument.
- Practice between 20 and 30 minutes each day.
- Stay relaxed when playing; tension is your worst enemy.
- Remember that a few minutes of quality practice is better than any minute of bad, unfocused practice. Only perfect practice makes perfect.
- Record yourself playing your instrument and evaluate things you did well and places where you could improve.
- Finish the practice session by playing something fun (maybe your favorite piece).

TIPS ON BREATHING

- Take a full breath using the syllable MAWH and drop the jaw.
- Relax when you take a breath; don't become tense when you inhale.
- Keep the flow of air moving and don't stop at the top of the inhale; this creates tension.
- Later, you can move from the MAWH syllable to the OH syllable when inhaling.
- You should feel your ribs expand outward; keep your shoulders down and relaxed.

THE PARTS OF YOUR INSTRUMENT

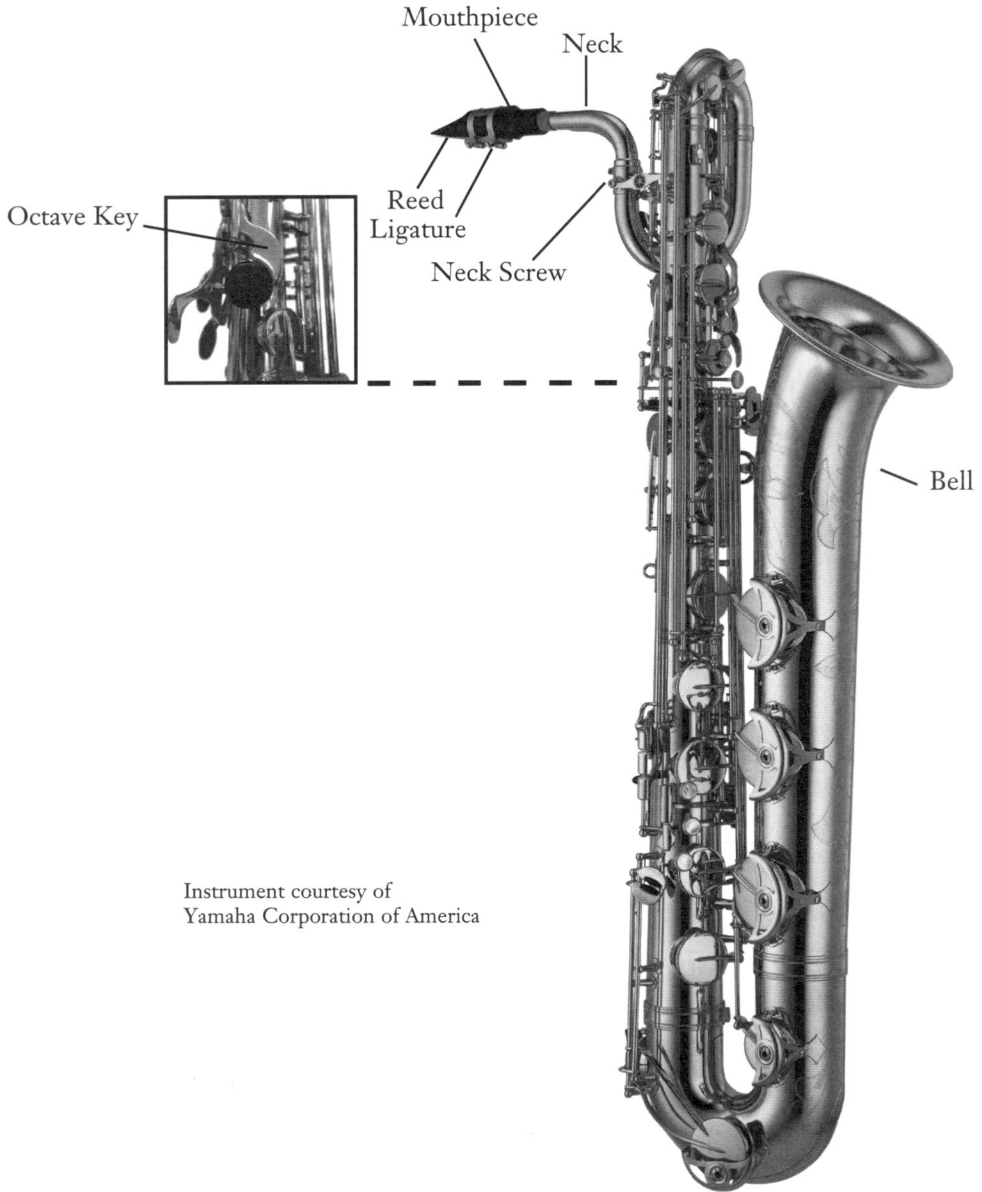

For a Start-up Clinic video on putting the baritone saxophone together, proper posture and playing position, embouchure formation and much more, go to:

www.habitsuniversal.com

YOUR FIRST SOUNDS ON THE MOUTHPIECE AND NECK

Baritone saxophonists should first learn to play B and A on the instrument. Then, learn to play (written fourth line) D to C; be tenacious about good hand position.

Music Theory Habits

Music symbols

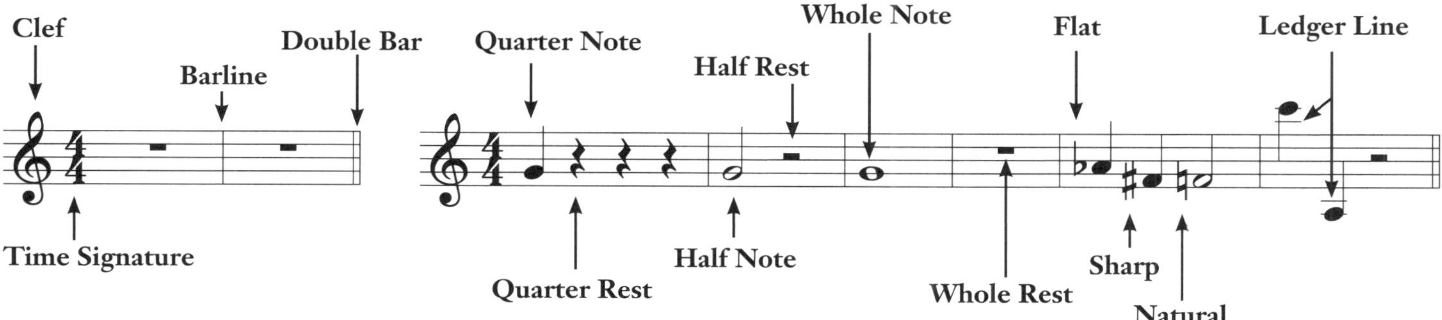

GLOSSARY OF TERMS

Clef A clef is a musical symbol used to indicate the pitch of written notes. Placed on a staff, it indicates the name and pitch of the notes on one of the lines or spaces.

Barline A barline is a single vertical line used to divide a musical staff into measures; barlines help us organize time.

Double Bar A double bar indicates the end of a section or appears at the conclusion of a piece of music.

Flat A flat sign (♭) is placed in front of a note to alter its pitch down one half step. It is also sometimes used as a courtesy reminder of the key signature.

Half Note A half note (𝅗𝅥) receives two beats if there is a 4 on the bottom of the time signature.

Half Rest A half rest (𝄼) receives two beats of silence if there is a 4 on the bottom of the time signature.

Ledger Line A ledger line is a short line added for notes above or below the range of a staff to extend the notes on the staff in both directions, higher and lower.

Natural A natural sign (♮) is placed in front of a note to cancel the effects of a sharp or a flat in the key signature or from a note occurring previously in the measure. A natural sign is also used as a courtesy reminder of the key signature.

Quarter Note A quarter note (♩) receives one beat if there is a 4 on the bottom of the time signature.

Quarter Rest A quarter rest (𝄽) receives one beat of silence if there is a 4 on the bottom of the time signature.

Sharp A sharp sign (♯) is placed in front of a note to alter its pitch up one half step. A sharp is also used as a courtesy reminder of the key signature.

Time Signature The time signature is an indication of time and rhythm following a clef, with the bottom number defining the beat as a division (what gets the beat) and the top number giving the number of beats in each bar.

Whole Note A whole note (𝅝) receives four beats if there is a 4 on the bottom of the time signature.

Whole Rest A whole rest (𝄻) receives four beats of silence if there is a 4 on the bottom of the time signature.

Music Theory Habits

Note Names

- Music is written with the first seven letters of the alphabet: A, B, C, D, E, F, G
- When going higher, once you get to "G," you start back over with "A"
- When going lower, once you get to "A," you continue down to "G, F, etc."
- This is what the musical staff looks like in treble clef:

Fill in the missing letters left-to-right going up the musical alphabet (or ascending):

A	____	____	____	____	____	____	A
B	____	____	____	____	____	____	B
F	____	____	____	____	____	____	F

Habits Rhythm Tree

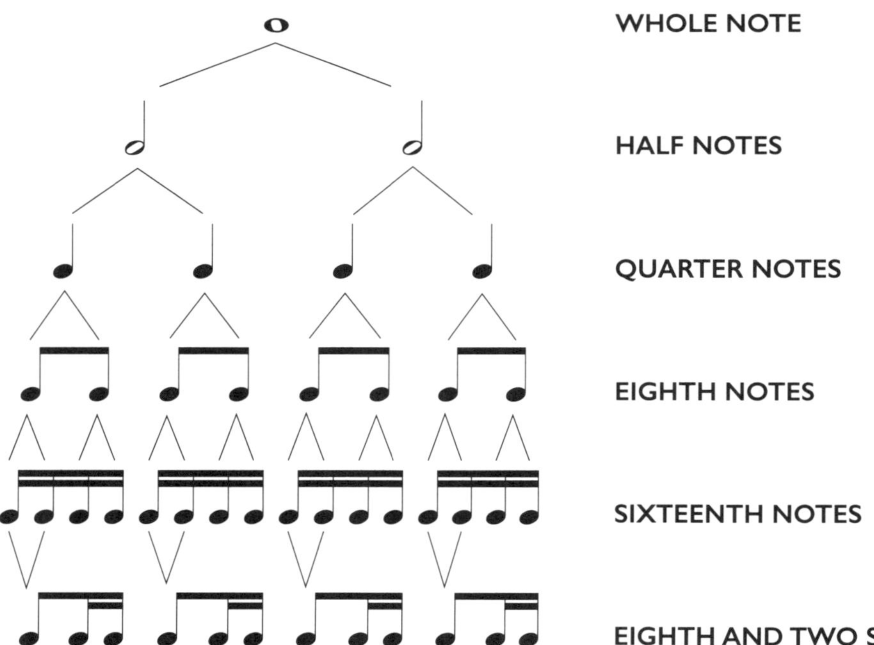

WHOLE NOTE

HALF NOTES

QUARTER NOTES

EIGHTH NOTES

SIXTEENTH NOTES

EIGHTH AND TWO SIXTEENTH NOTES

I. First Days Rhythm Charts

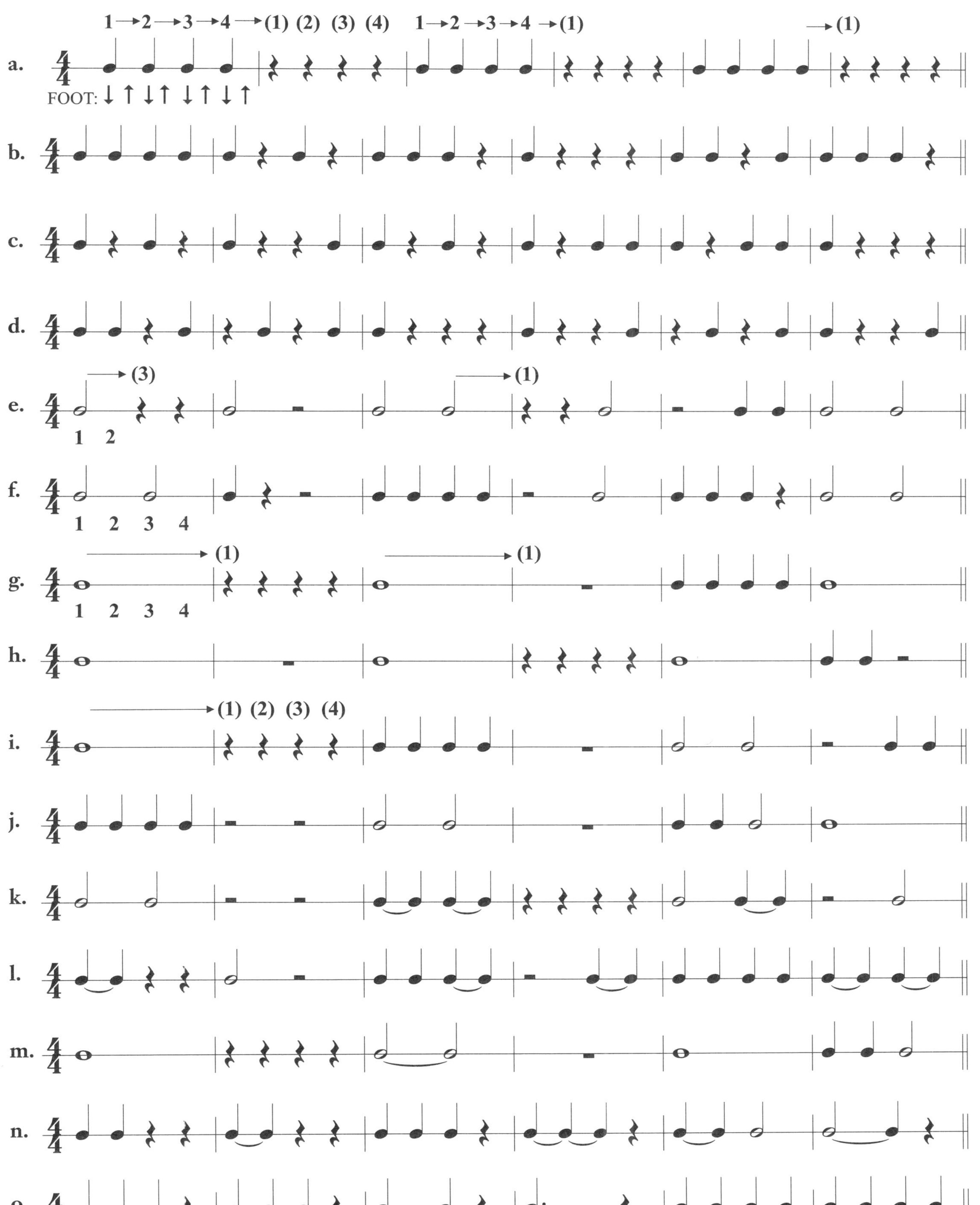

II. First Days Solfege

Your first five notes

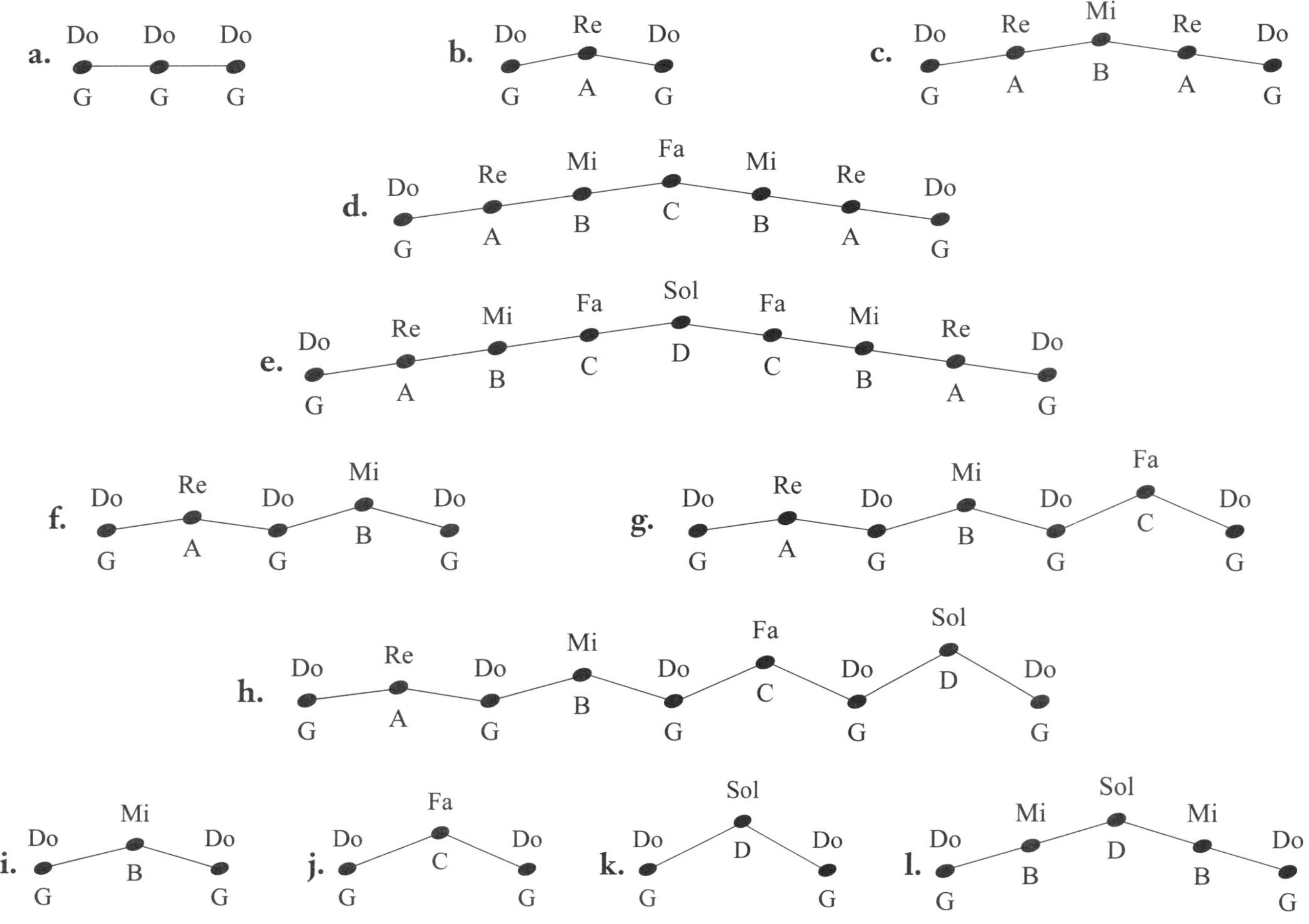

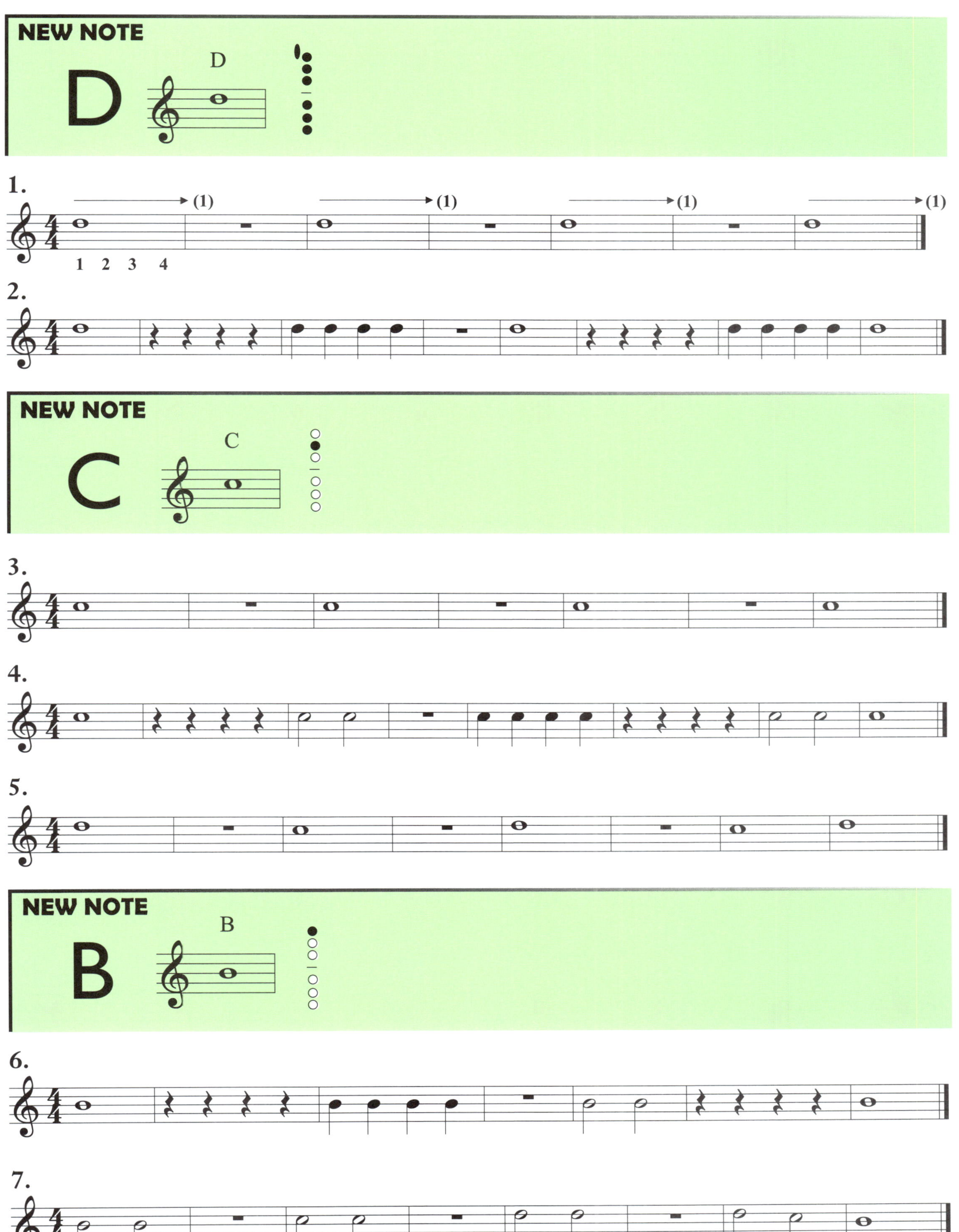
NEW NOTE
D
D
1.
(1)
(1)
(1)
(1)
1 2 3 4
2.
NEW NOTE
C
C
3.
4.
5.
NEW NOTE
B
B
6.
7.

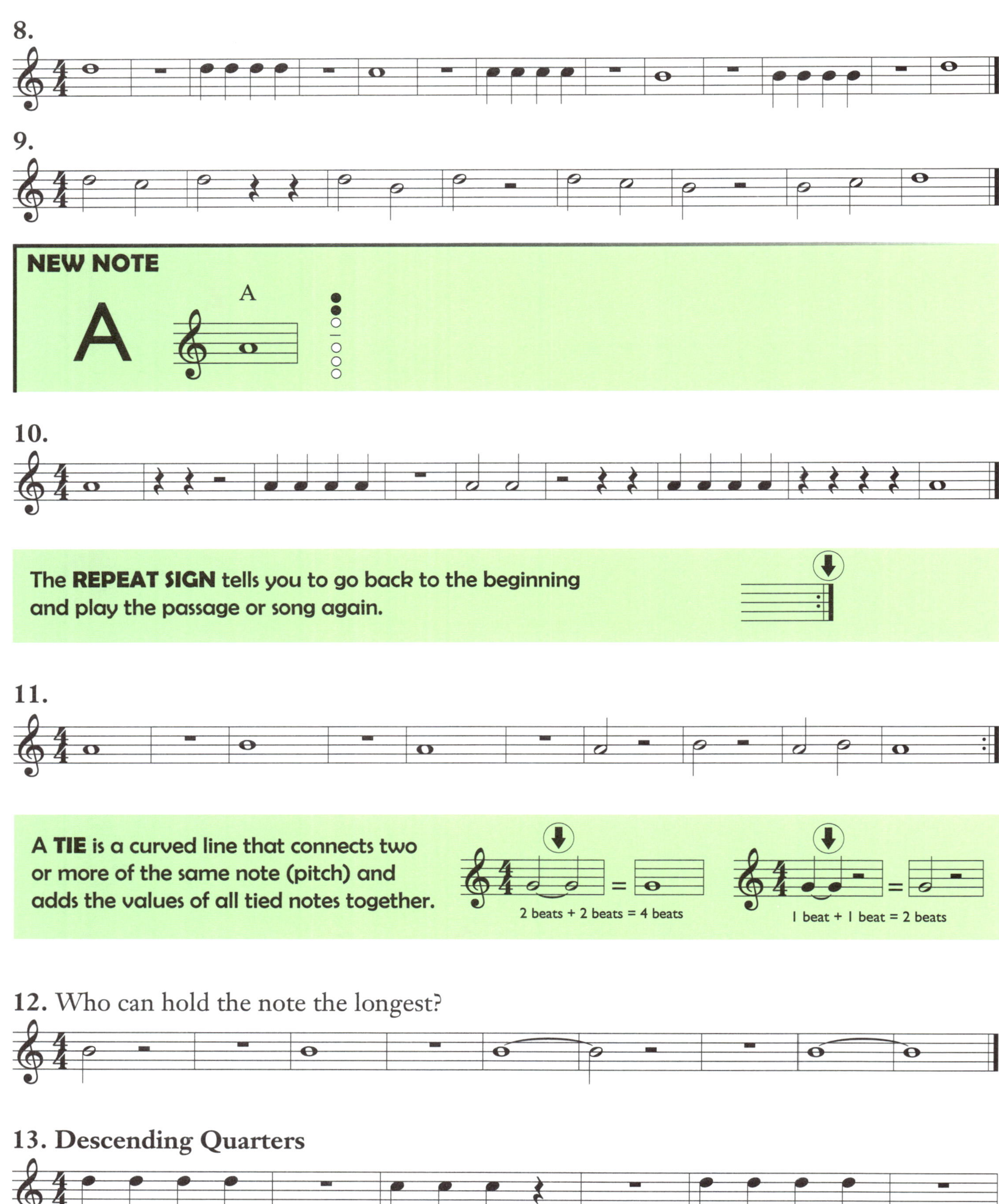
8.
9.
NEW NOTE
A
A
10.
The REPEAT SIGN tells you to go back to the beginning and play the passage or song again.
11.
A TIE is a curved line that connects two or more of the same note (pitch) and adds the values of all tied notes together.
2 beats + 2 beats = 4 beats
1 beat + 1 beat = 2 beats
12. Who can hold the note the longest?
13. Descending Quarters

The **KEY SIGNATURE** appears just after the clef sign and tells you which notes to play in the key. This is your key of **G MAJOR (CONCERT B-FLAT)**, and tells you that F is sharp.

14. New Note G

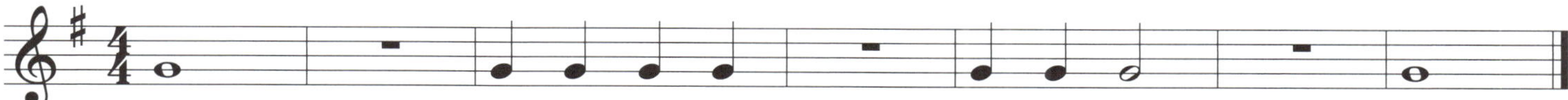

15. Step Up, Step Down

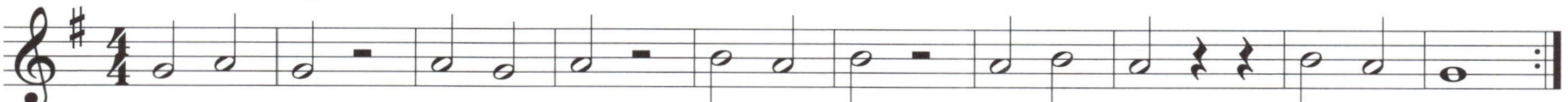

16. Pentastic

17. Concert B♭ (Your G) Pentascale - Playing Test #1

A **SOLO** is a composition or passage for one performer.

A **DUET** is a composition or passage for two performers.

18. Hot Bundt Cakes Duet

19. Leap Frog

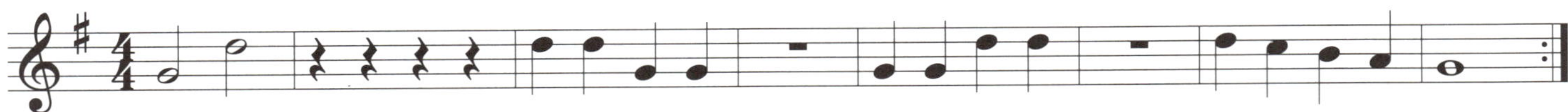

A **SLUR** is indicated by a curved line connecting two or more different pitches. When performing, tongue the first note of the slur and then connect the second or additional notes by not tonguing them.

tongue tongue tongue slur tongue tongue tongue tongue slur slur

20. First Lip Slur

21. Give Me Five

22. Don't Skip It

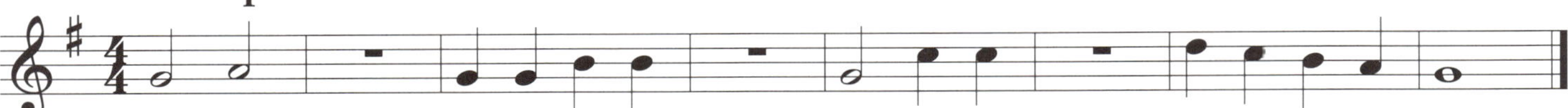

COMMON TIME is another name for $\frac{4}{4}$ and is indicated with the following symbol:

23. Go Tell Aunty

24. Lamb Chops

25. Rhythm Prep for Playing Test #2

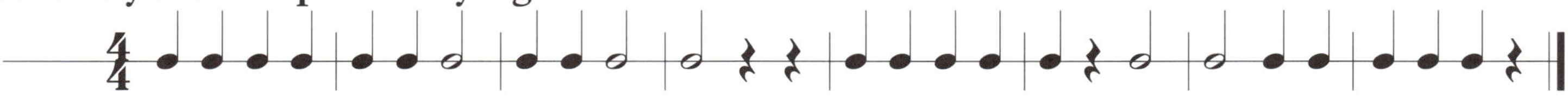

26. Jubilee - Playing Test #2

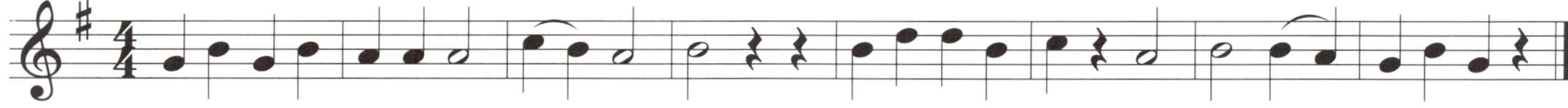

The **BREATH MARK** tells you when to breathe.
(NB) means no breath.

27. Skips

28. Beethoven's Joy

L. van Beethoven

29. Brightly Shining

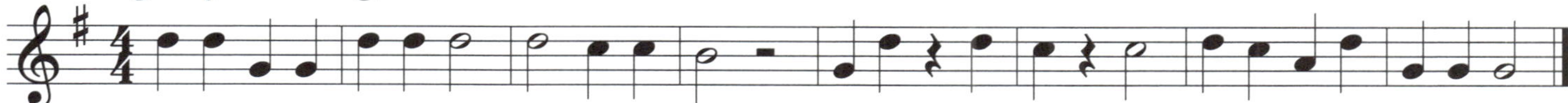

30. Rhythm Prep

31. I Like It

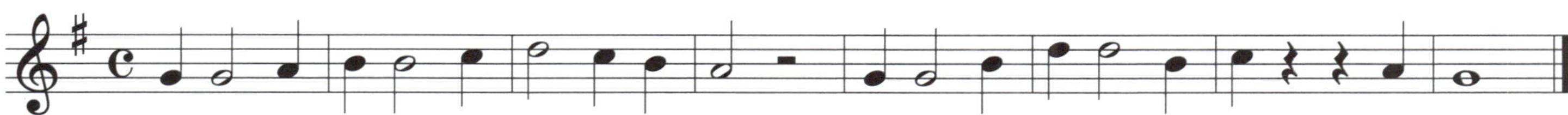

32. Dreidel Spinning Top

33. The Good King - Playing Test #3

NEW NOTE

E

34. New Note E

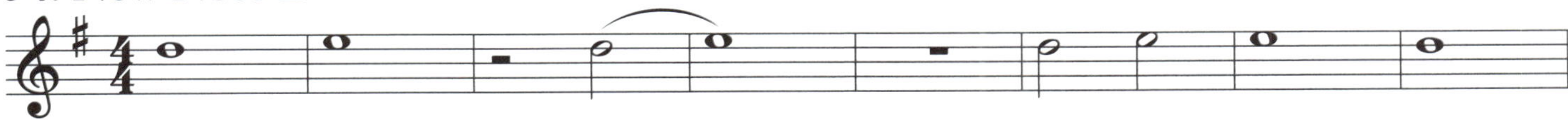

35. Finger Roll

36. Two-Note Slurs

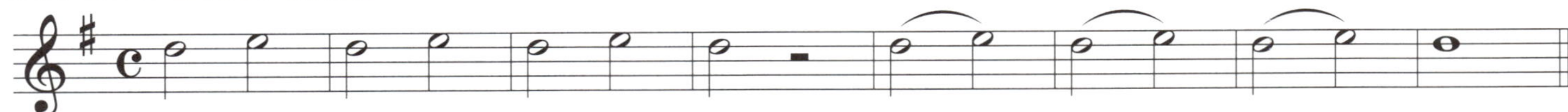

DYNAMICS refers to the volume in which we play. Dynamics can be loud (called **FORTE** and indicated by the letter *f*) or soft (called **PIANO** and indicated by the letter *p*).

37. Good Pierrot

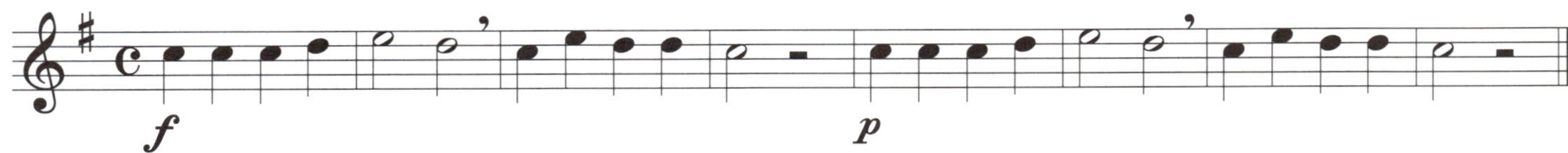

38. Shining Stars

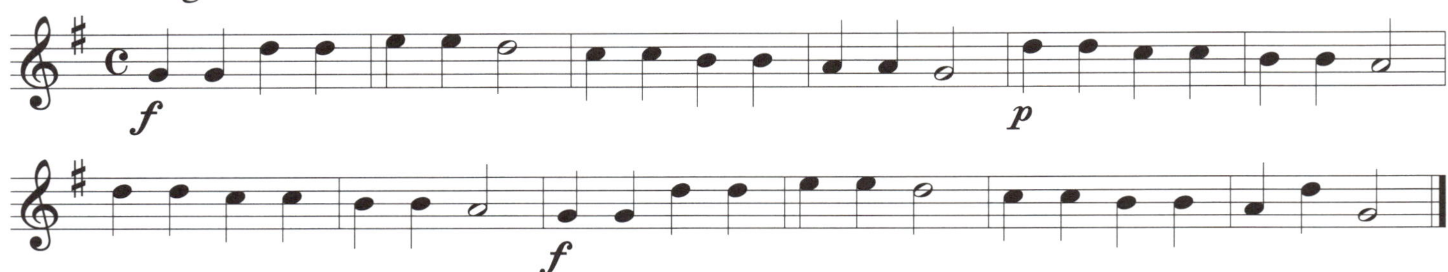

39. It's Raining

A **THEME AND VARIATION** is a form of music that begins with a melody (the theme) and is then altered or changed in some way throughout the piece.

40. The Bridge - Theme

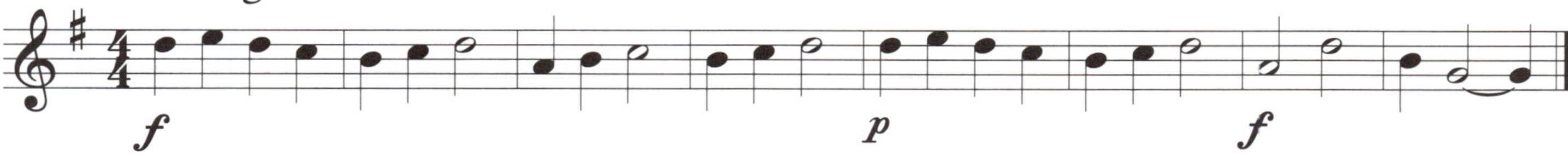

The top number in $\frac{2}{4}$ **Time** tells you that there are two beats per measure; the bottom number tells you that the quarter note gets one beat.

41. Suspension Bridge - Variation

42. New Note F♯

43. Lost Polly

An **ARTICULATION** indicates how a note should be played and is applied at the beginning of the note.

LEGATO means smooth and connected, and is indicated by a dash or a **TENUTO** marking (ten.).

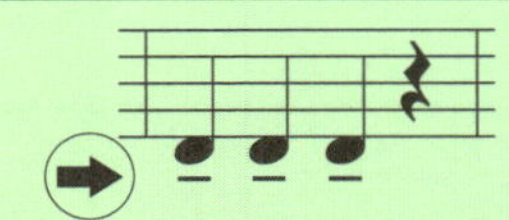

STACCATO means a separated, detached style and generally means to put space between the notes.

44. Sound and Space

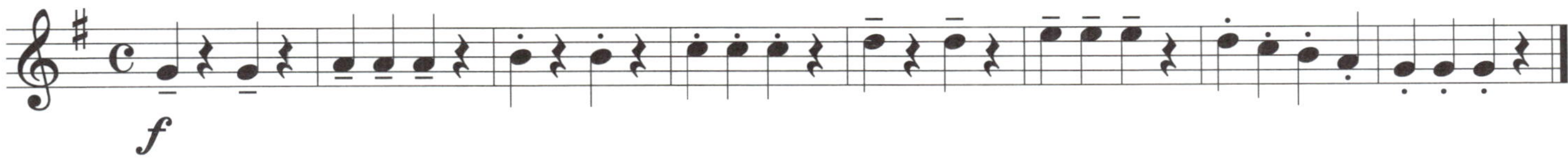

45. Up and Down the Ladder

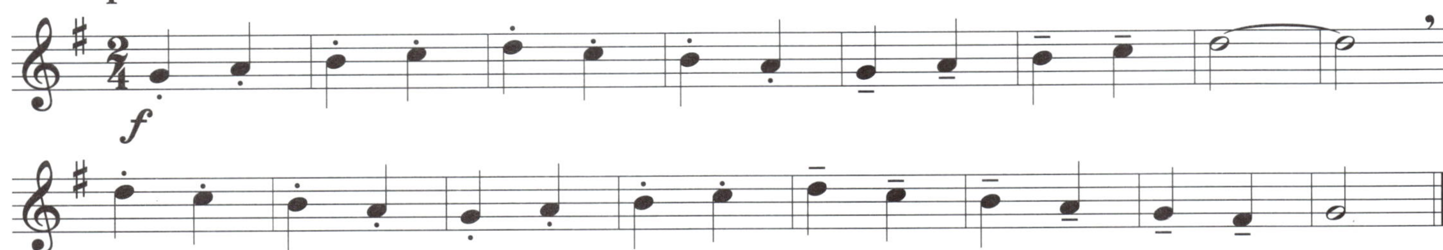

A **CRESCENDO** means to get gradually louder and is indicated by cresc. or < .
A **DIMINUENDO** or **DECRESCENDO** means to get gradually softer and is indicated by dim. or > .

46. Crescendo/Diminuendo

An **INTERVAL** is the distance between two notes. The interval on the same note is **UNISON** and then we use numbers to indicate interval distance. An eighth is also called an **OCTAVE**.

47. Fun with Thirds - Playing Test #4

NEW NOTE

ACCIDENTAL: A note not in the key that is represented by a sharp (♯), flat (♭) or natural (♮) sign.

48. An Accident Ready to Happen *(The accidental stays in effect until the barline)*

Your new key signature is **A MAJOR** (Concert C) and tells you that F, C and G are sharp.

49. Rain

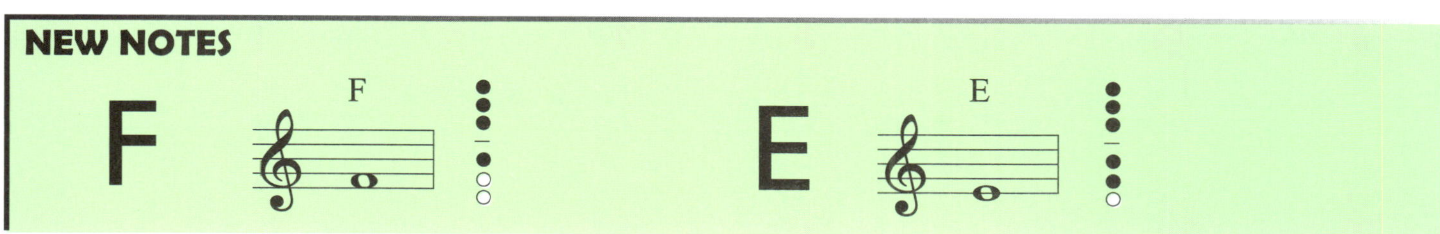

50. Lip Slur #2

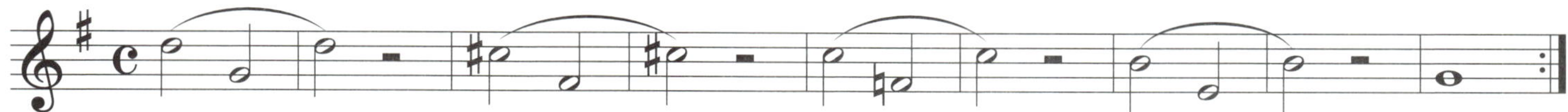

51. The Other Ladder

52. Half Way Down

MEZZO FORTE (*mf*) means moderately loud. **MEZZO PIANO** (*mp*) means moderately soft.

53. Down to the Bottom - Playing Test #5

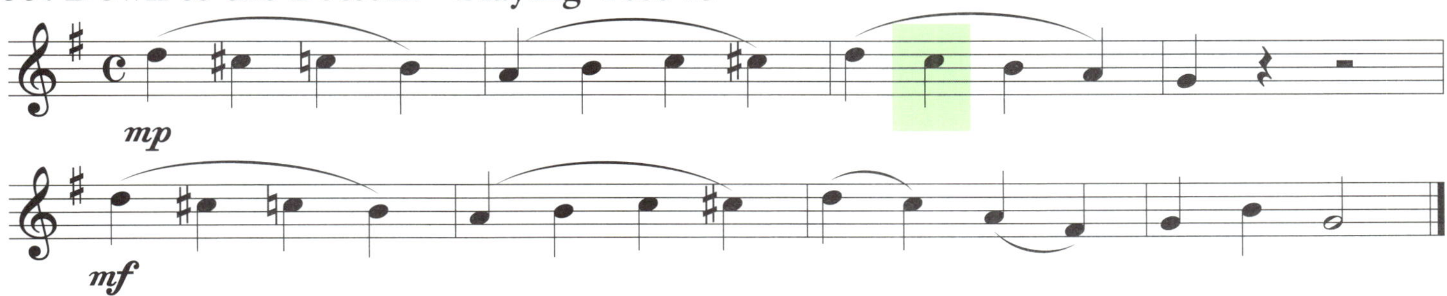

An **ACCENT** placed on a note means to play with a stronger attack and generally means to put about 30% more air at the front of the note.

54. Taco Truck

NEW NOTE

B♭

55. Interval Study

56. Goodnight, Moonlight

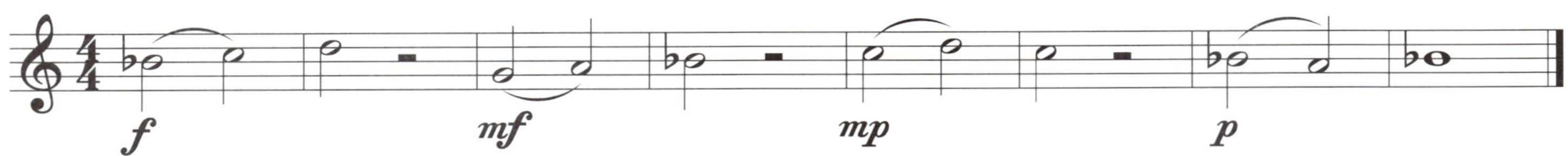

EIGHTH NOTES receive a half beat if there is a 4 on the bottom of the time signature.

57. Rhythm Study

58.

59.

The **TONALITY OF MUSIC** is usually in a **MAJOR** key or a **MINOR** key. We generally hear music in major as being "happy" and music in minor as sounding "sad."

60. Oopsy Lou - Playing Test #6

61. Finger Pattern Exercise

62. This Old Man Fell Down

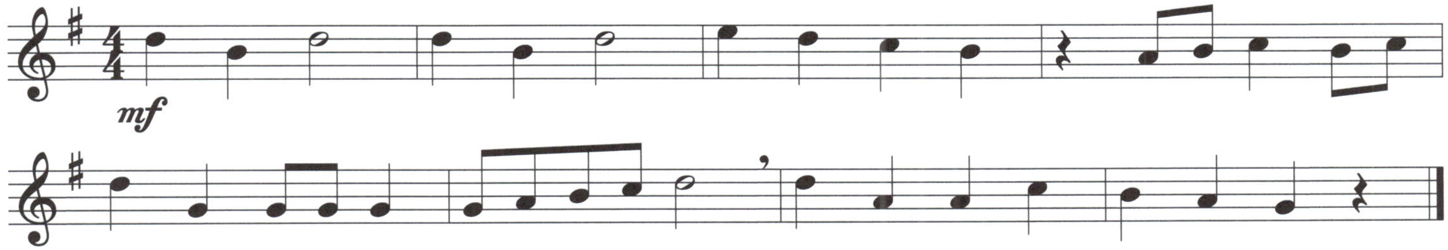

DIVISI (div.) means that two notes appear on the music and we call this "split parts" or divided.

UNISON (unis.) is when everyone is playing the same pitch.

63. Long, Long Ago

Your new key signature is **C MAJOR** (Concert E-flat) with no sharps or flats.

64. On Deck

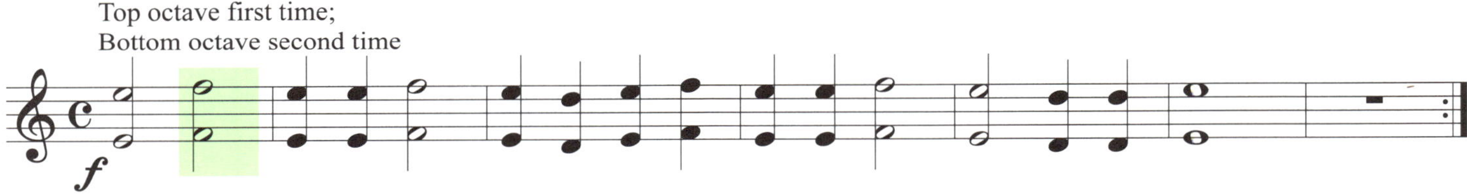

A **FERMATA** is a hold or pause and means to hold a note or rest longer than its normal duration.

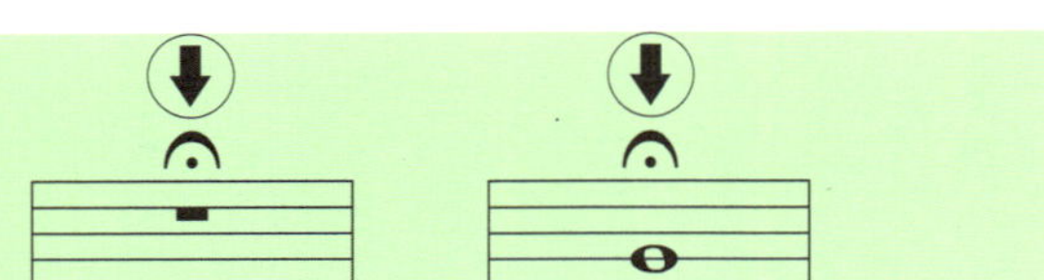

65. Japanese Folk Song

The top number in $\frac{3}{4}$ **TIME** tells you that there are three beats per measure; the bottom number tells you that the quarter note gets the beat.

A **DOT** adds half of the value to the note that it is on. For example, if a dot is placed on a half note, then a **DOTTED HALF NOTE** receives three beats because 2+1=3.

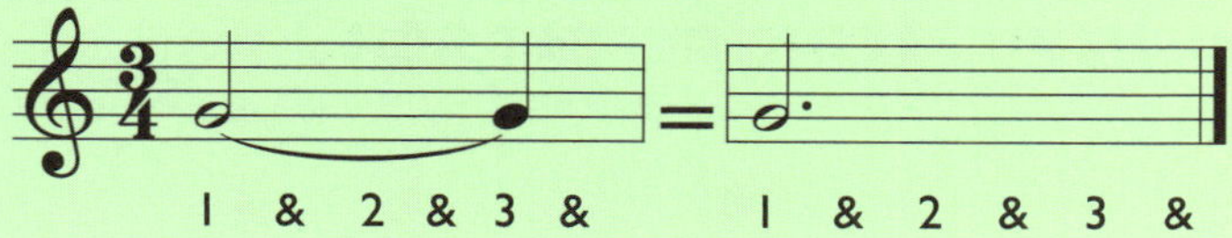

66. Rhythm Chart

A **PICKUP NOTE** (or anacrusis) occurs before the first full measure and contains one or more notes. Often, the final measure is missing an equal number of beats as the pick-ups.

67. The Banks O' Doon - Playing Test #7

Scottish Tune

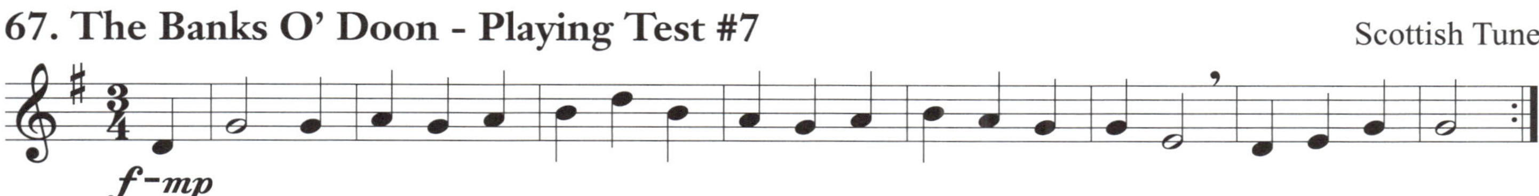

A **MULTI-MEASURE REST** means to rest, while counting the indicated number.

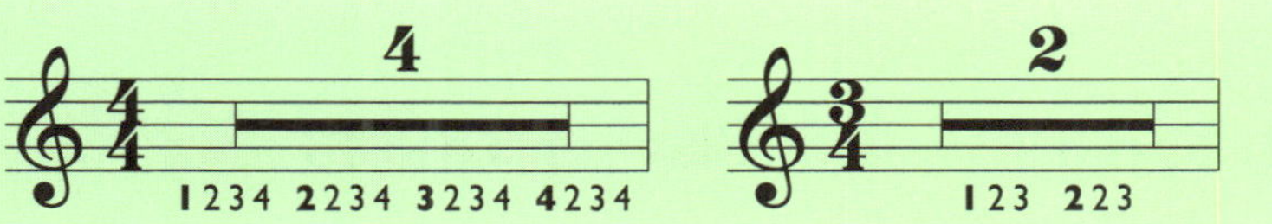

68. Peer Gynt

E. Grieg

When performing a piece with a **FIRST AND SECOND ENDING**, play the first ending the first time through and then skip the first ending and play the second ending the second time through.

A **RIGHT-FACING** or **FORWARD FACING REPEAT SIGN** shows where to return to repeat the music.

69. The Flying Showman

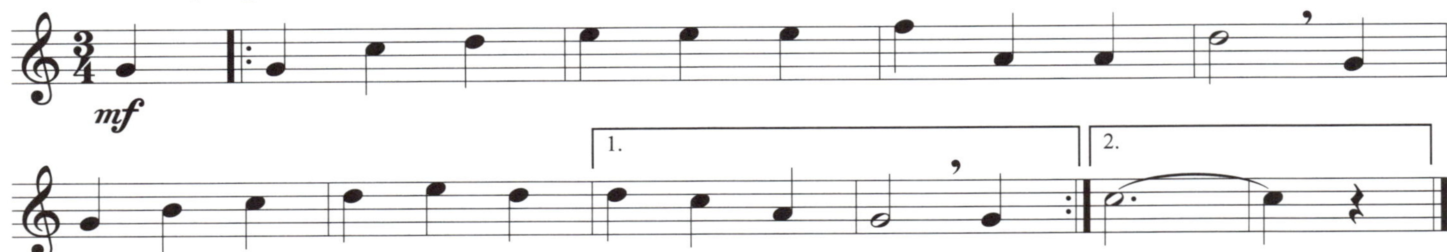

TEMPO MARKINGS are words that indicate a general speed to the music.

Allegro - rapid; lively.
Andante - moderately slow, but moving.
Largo - very slow.

70. Lovely Branches

Allegro

71. Sarah's Waltz - Playing Test #8

Andante

A **ONE-MEASURE REPEAT** means to repeat the previous measure. 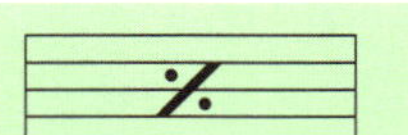

72. Mahler Symphony #1 (Third Movement)

Largo G. Mahler

73. Interval Exercise

74. Register Exercise

75. Whole Tone Scale - Playing Test #9

Your new key signature is **D MAJOR** (Concert F) and tells you that F and C are sharp.

76. Caroline's Song

77. Aura Lee

78. Old St. Nick

79. The Long Jump

80. Concert E♭ (Your C) Pentascale - Playing Test #10

81. Articulation Study

A **RITARDANDO** (rit.) or **RALLENTANDO** (rall.) means to get gradually slower.

A **CHORALE** is a slow, beautiful piece. Many bands play chorales as part of their warm-up.

82. Chorale Tune #1 - Full Band

REHEARSAL MARKINGS are indicated by putting a box around a measure number or by putting a box around a letter. Rehearsal markings help musicians find a logical starting point in a longer piece of music.

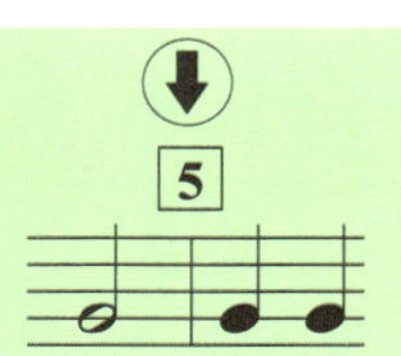

STYLE MARKINGS are like tempo markings, but are intended to convey mood, feeling, and style.

83. Angels - Full Band

Arranged by Leslie Gilreath

D.C. AL FINE means to go back to the beginning, repeat the musical material, and play to the Fine, which means "to the finish."

84. Bring a Torch - Full Band

Arranged by Leslie Gilreath

Moderato ♩ = 108

mf · *mp* · *Fine* · 9 · *D.C. al Fine*

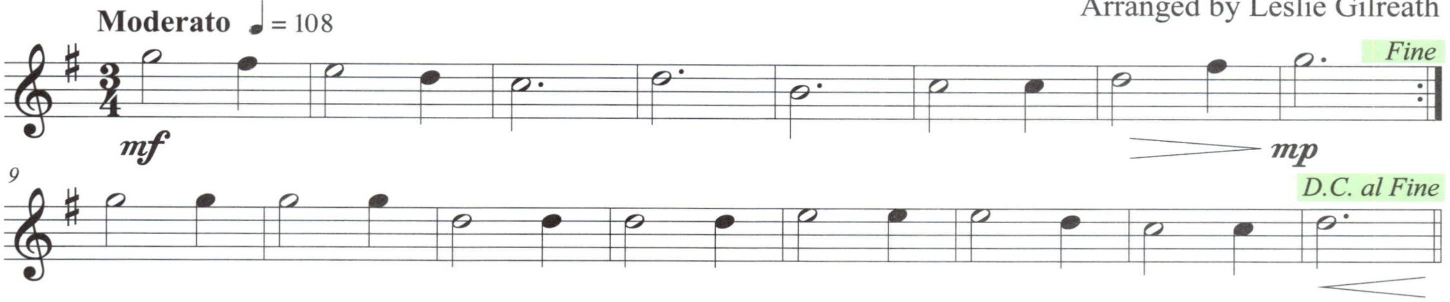

85. Good King - Full Band

Arranged by Leslie Gilreath

Maestoso ♩ = 120

f · 5 · *mp* · 9 · 2 · *mp* · 13 · *f* · *mp* · *f*

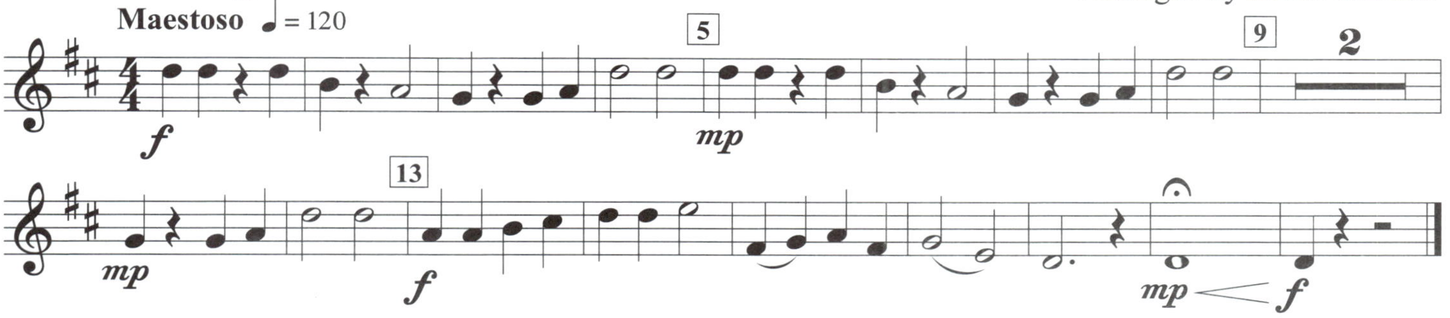

86. Concert B♭ (Your G) Scale - Playing Test #11

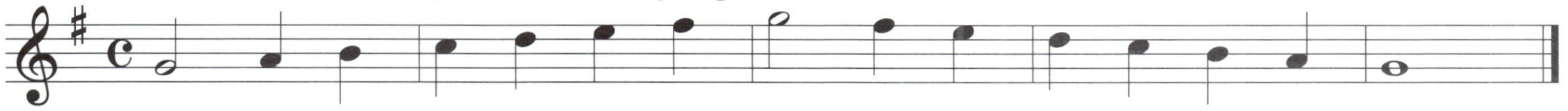

87. High Interval Study

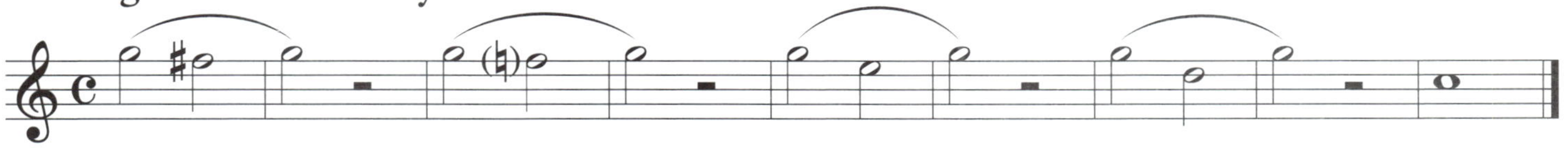

A **TRIO** is a musical passage written for three performers.

88. Chorale Trio

J. S. Bach

89. On the Double

Play the lower octave on the repeat.

90. Jamaican Folk Song

EIGHTH NOTES and **EIGHTH RESTS** can appear as single notes and rests. Eighth rests are a half beat of silence.

91. Rhythm Prep

92. Space Cadets

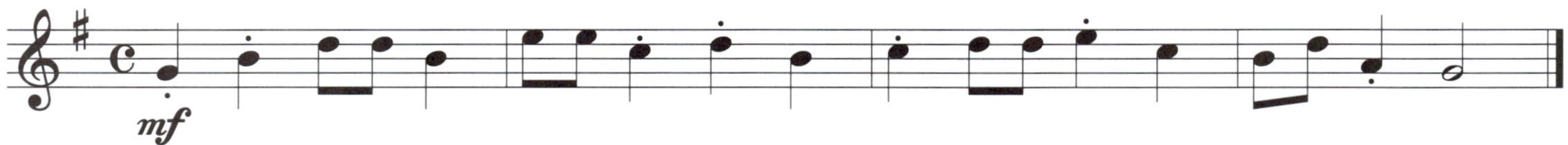

93. Ghost in the Attic - Playing Test #12

94. Dorian Dance

SOSTENUTO means "sustained."

95. March Slav

OFF-THE-BEAT EIGHTH NOTES: Single eighth notes can also be played off the beat.

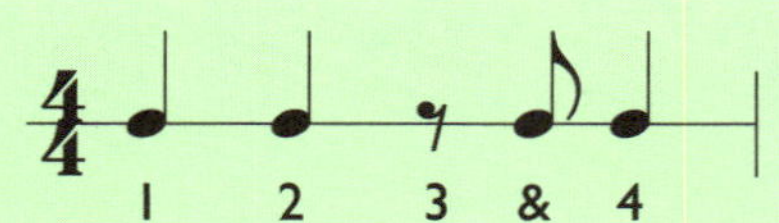

96. Rhythm Chart

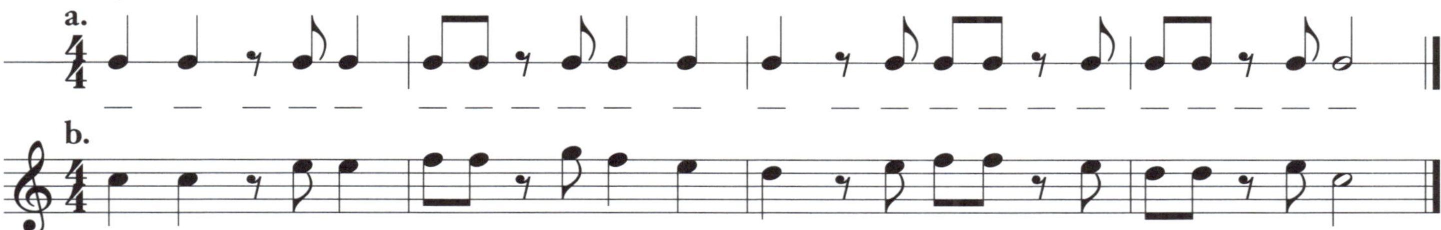

97. This Is the Story

98. Calypso

99. Low Interval Study

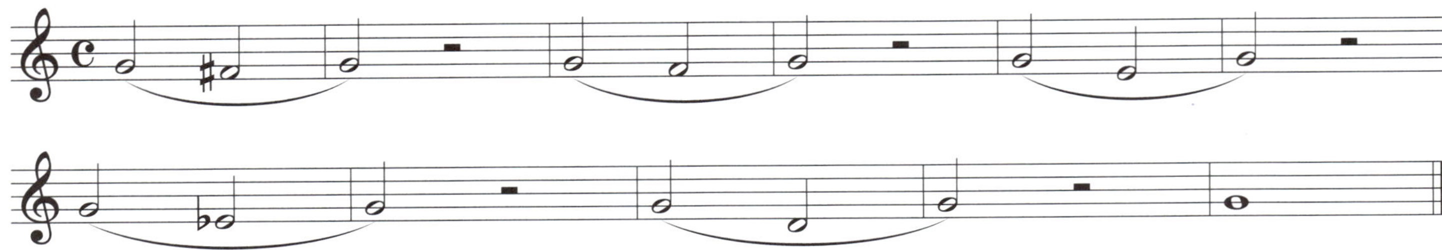

100. Down in the Basement

101. Scottish Folk Song

102. Carnival of Venice

103. Russian Folk Song

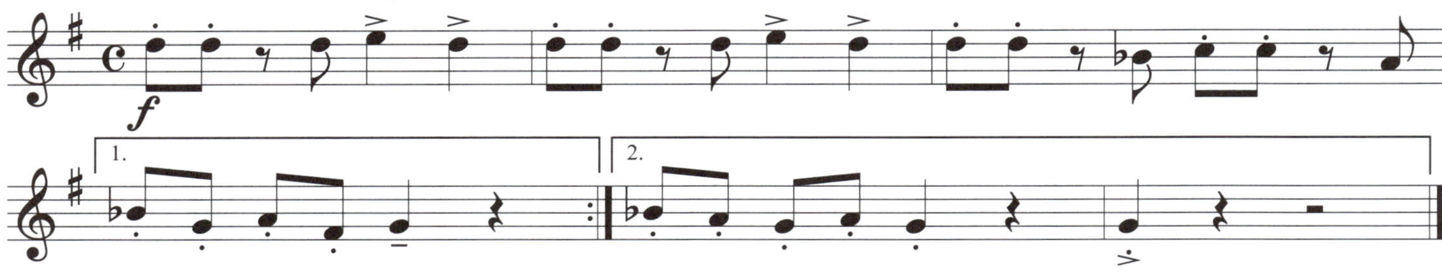

BASIC DAILY WARM-UP

A. Interval Study

B. Whole Tone Scale

C. Low Concert F Scale

D. Lip Slur #2

E. Chorale Tune #1

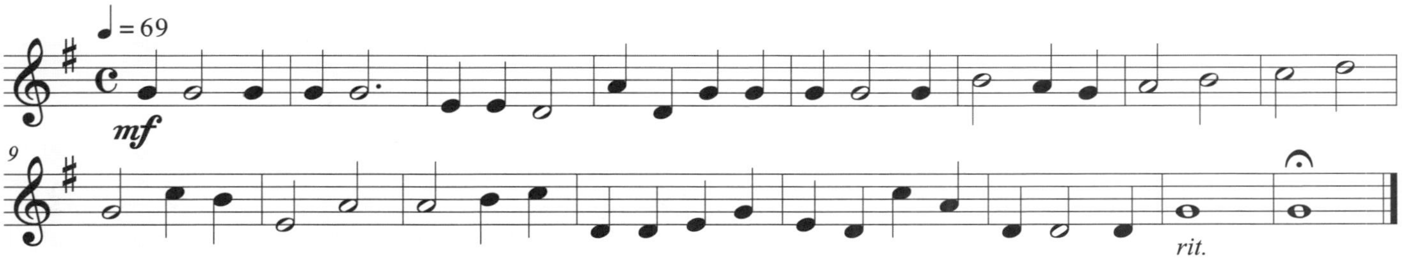

♩ = 69

mf

rit.

Remember that $\frac{6}{4}$ is nothing more than $\frac{4}{4}$ with two additional beats - we simply count to six in each measure.

104. Chorale Tune

J. S. Bach

105. Song of the Sea

In a time signature where the lower number is 4, a **DOTTED QUARTER NOTE** receives 1½ beats because the dot adds half of the value of the note to the note (1+½ = 1½). When playing dotted quarter notes, internally hear three clicks, which are the subdivided eighth notes.

106. Rhythm Prep

107. Rhythm Prep

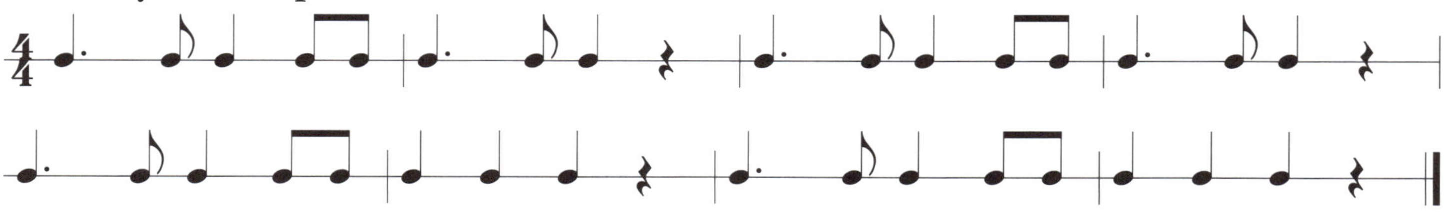

108. All Together

109. On the Mountain - Playing Test #13

110. New World Symphony Melody

A. Dvořák

111. Largo from The New World Symphony - Full Band

A. Dvořák

D.S. AL FINE means to go back to the sign (dal segno), repeat the musical material, and play to the Fine, which means "to the finish."

112. Ode to Joy - Full Band

L. van Beethoven

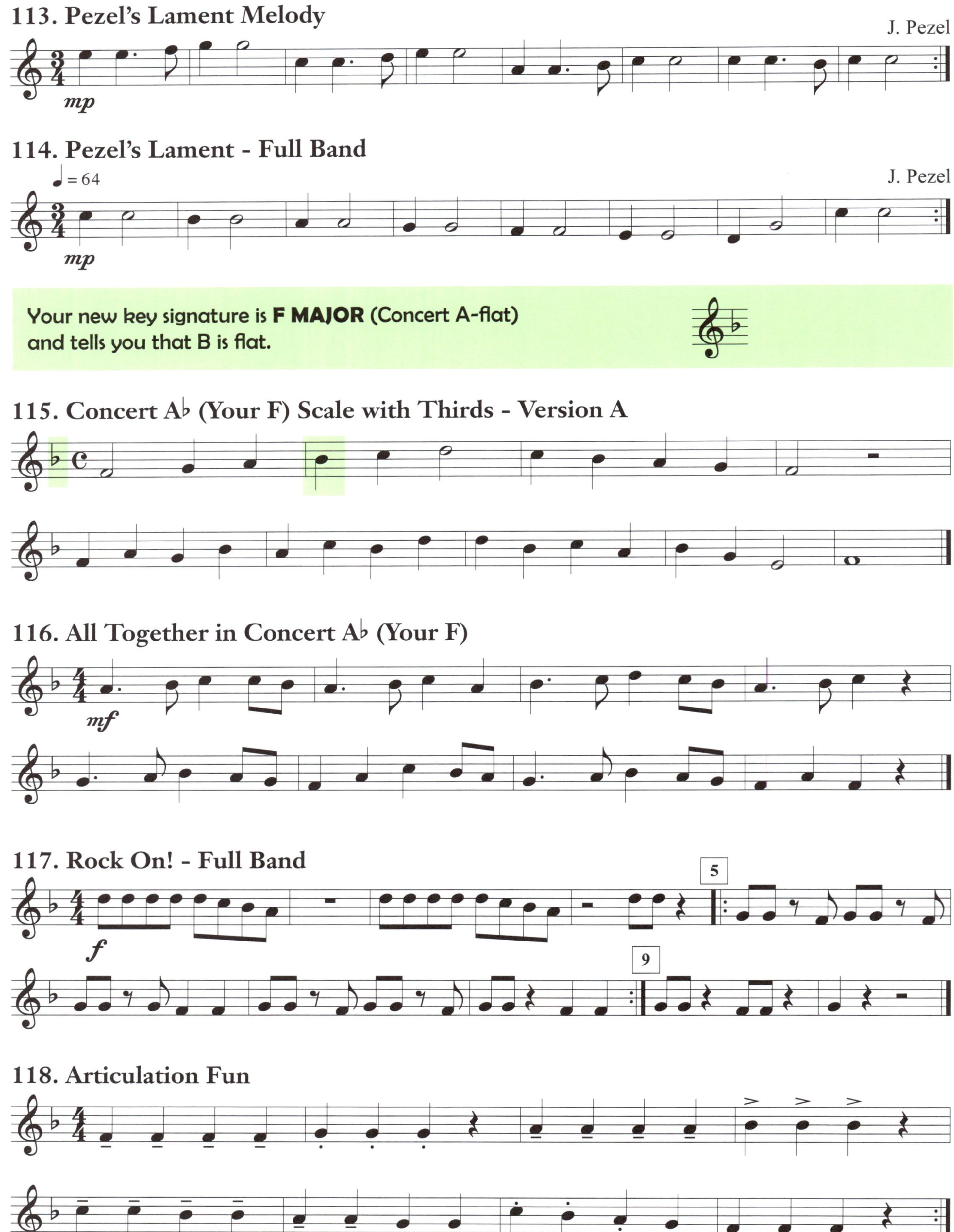
113. Pezel's Lament Melody
J. Pezel
mp
114. Pezel's Lament - Full Band
♩ = 64
J. Pezel
mp
Your new key signature is F MAJOR (Concert A-flat)
and tells you that B is flat.
115. Concert A♭ (Your F) Scale with Thirds - Version A
116. All Together in Concert A♭ (Your F)
mf
117. Rock On! - Full Band
f
5
9
118. Articulation Fun

123. Lip Slur #4

124. Tchaikovsky's Fourth - Playing Test #14

P. Tchaikovsky

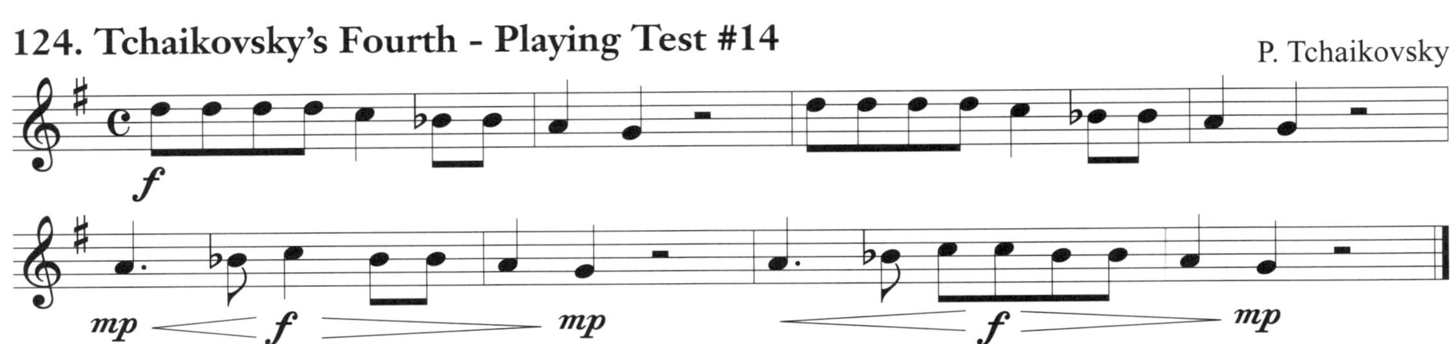

125. Austrian Folk Song

126. Lip Slur #5

127. Kick It Out

128. Concert A♭ (Your F) Pentascale

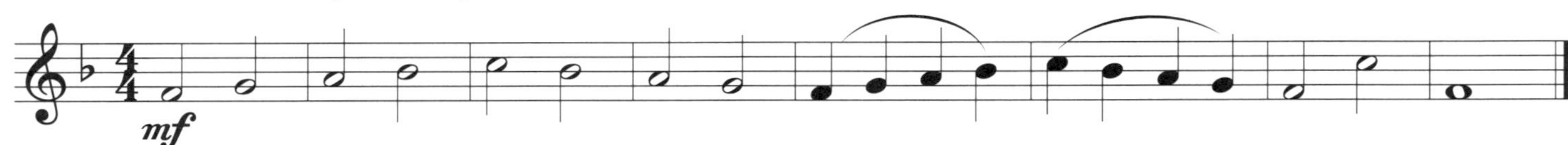

129. Snow Flakes

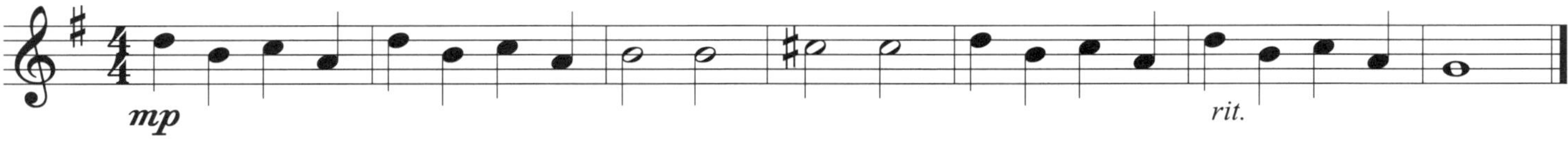

130. The Big Monster

131. Simple Gifts - Playing Test #15

Shaker Melody

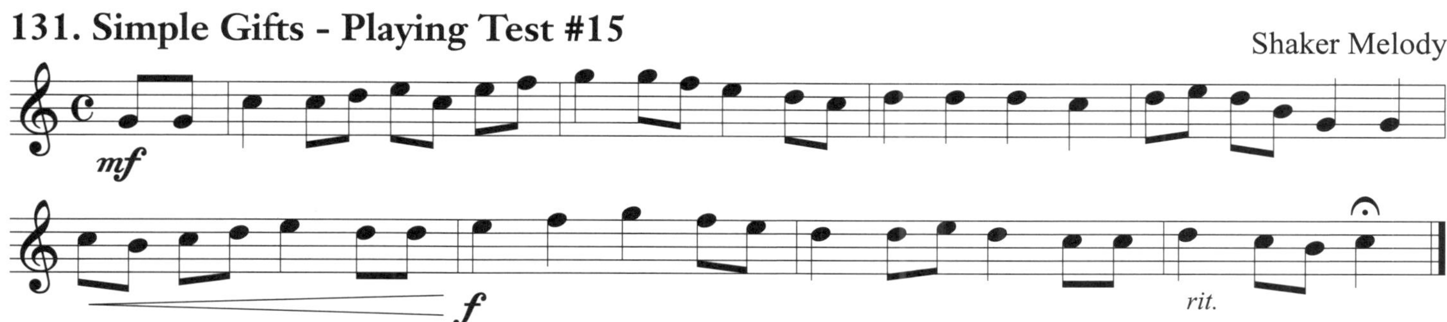

132. Swan Lake

P. Tchaikovsky

133. Shepherd's Hey

English Folk Song

134. Finlandia

J. Sibelius

135. Concert F (Your D) Pentascale

136. Concert E♭ (Your C) with Thirds - Playing Test #16

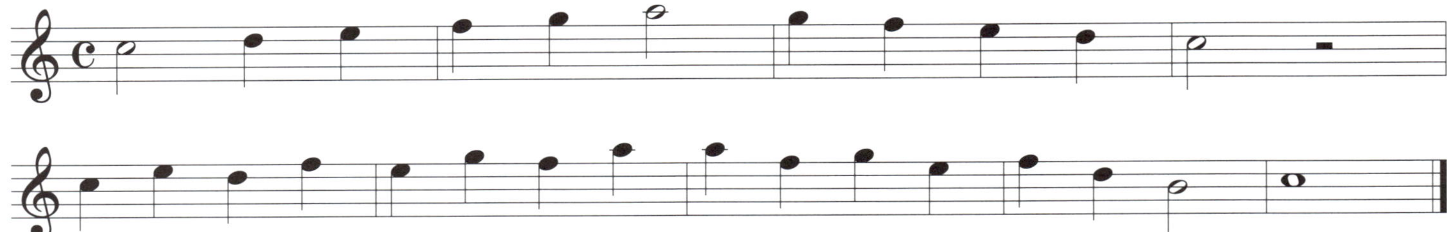

137. Welsh Folk Song

Traditional

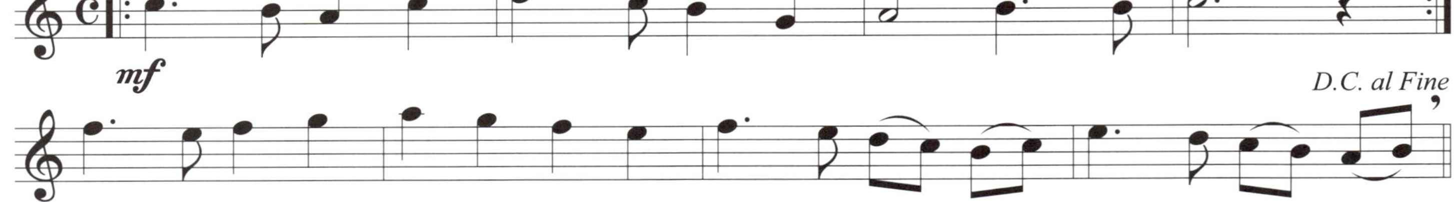

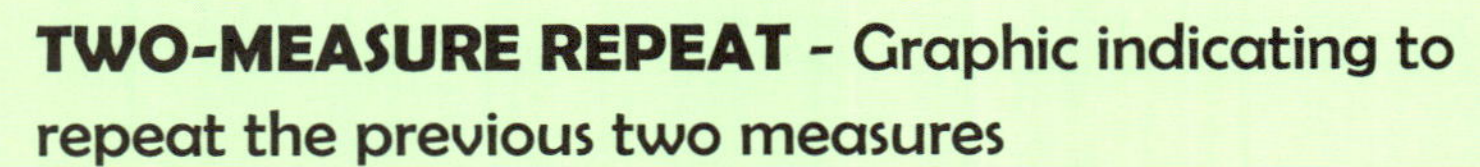
TWO-MEASURE REPEAT - Graphic indicating to repeat the previous two measures

MARCATO (marc.) - with emphasis on the front part of the note

FORTISSIMO (*ff*) - Very loud (with good tone)

PIANISSIMO (*pp*) - Very soft (with fast air)

138. Mahler Symphony #1 Ending

G. Mahler

139. Brahms Symphony #1

J. Brahms

MUSICAL PHRASE - A musical sentence.

140. Renaissance Tune

141. Rhythm Prep

142. Latin Blues
f
NEW NOTES
G♯
G♯
G♯
G♯
143. New Note G♯
144. March
ff
5
f
13
21
mp
29
f
145. Lip Slur #6

INTERMEDIATE DAILY WARM-UP
A. Interval Study 2
B. Whole Tone Add-On
(G♯)
C. The Attack Pattern
D. Concert B♭ (Your G) with Thirds
E. Lip Slur #5
F. Five-Step Scale Study #2
G. Chorale Tune #3 - Early One Morning
mf
6
f
11
p
mf
Chromatic Ladder
♭'s go
C
B
A♯
B♭
A
G♯
A♭
G
F♯
G♭
F
E
D♯
E♭
D
C♯
D♭
C
♯'s go

146. Descending Intervals

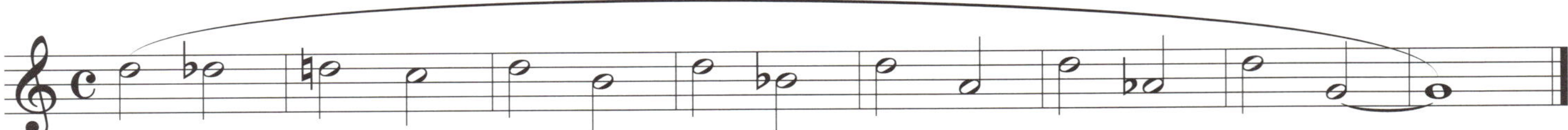

147. Chromatic Scale - Playing Test #17

148. Slippery Slope

149. Enharmonic Lambs
a.
b.
150. Finger Twister #1
151. Finger Twister #2
152. Finger Twister #3
153. A Young Girl's Heart - Playing Test #18
mp
mf
mp
f
rit.
mp

154. Auld Lang Syne
mf
155. Rhythm Study
a.
b.
c.
156. You Are My Friend
mp
f
mp
157. Armenian Folk Song
mf
f
mp

158. Carmen

G. Bizet

159. Concert A♭ (Your F) Scale with Thirds - Version B

160. Lazy Days - Playing Test #19

161. Concert C (Your A) Scale with Thirds - Version A

162. Concert F (Your D) Scale with Thirds

163. Haitian Folk Song

164. Rhythm Prep

a.

b.

c.

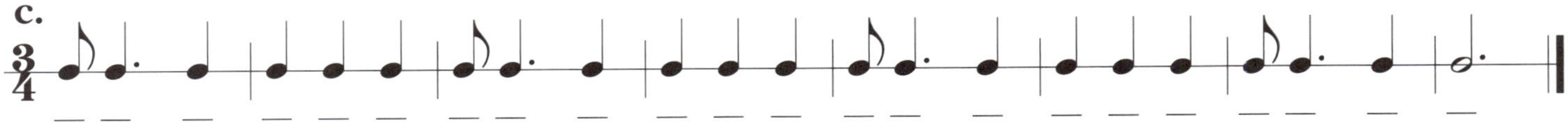

165. Southwest Saga

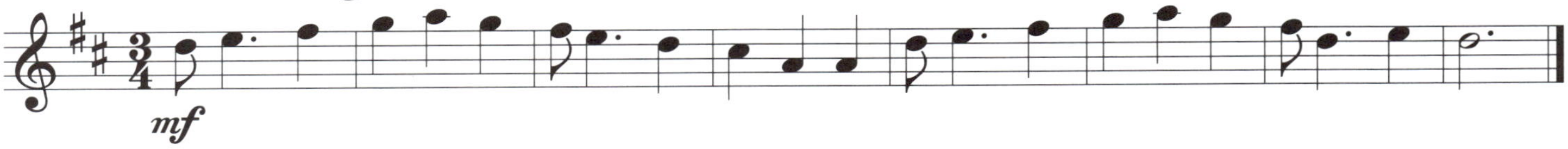

166. Southwest Saga (Variation)

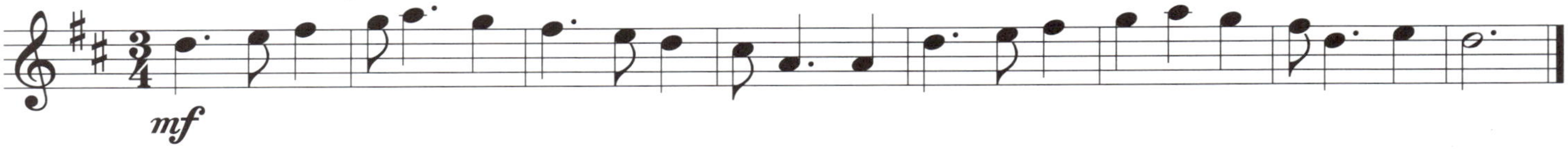

167. Up Four, Down Four

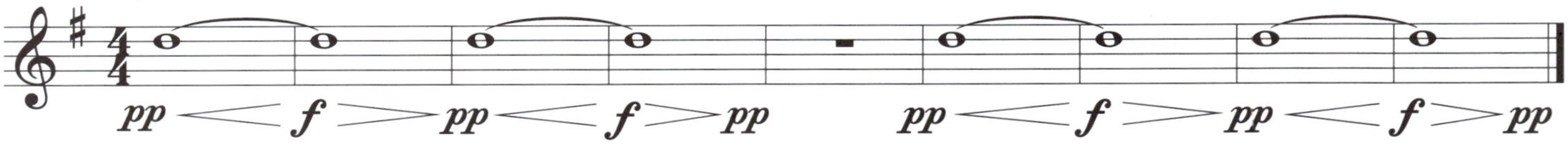

A musical sentence (phrase) can have dynamic shape.

168. Thomas Whistles *You determine the appropriate dynamic level, but balance down.*

169. Ye Banks and Braes
What dynamic shape do you think could be used with this song?
Scottish Tune
rit.
170. Molly Malone - Playing Test #20
Irish Tune
mp
f
mp
f
rit.
171. This Train
f
172. Arpeggios and Chords
f
(I)
(IV)
(V)
(I)
CUT TIME (¢) means that the conductor can show just two beats per bar instead of four.
173. William Tell
G. Rossini
C or ¢
f 1 2 & 3 4 1 2 & 3 4
mp
f
174. Tchaikovsky Piano Concerto
P. Tchaikovsky
mf
mp
f

175. Take Me Out to the Ball Game
9
17
25
176. Concert C (Your A) Scale with Thirds - Version B
177. In the Bleak Midwinter
G. Holst
178. I Heard the Bells
179. Scarborough Fair
English Ballad

ADVANCED DAILY WARM-UP

A. Ascending Intervals

B. Whole Tone Scale with P1 and P2 in Quarter Notes

C. B, B, T, and T (Balance, Blend, Tuning, and Tone)

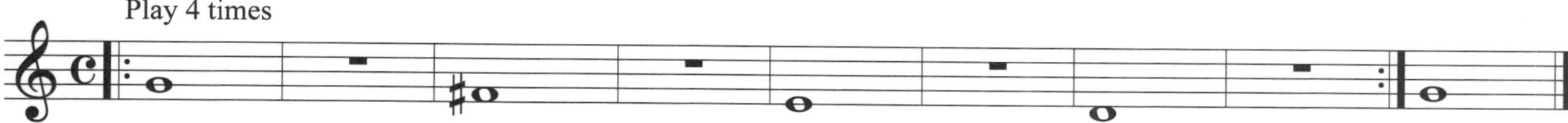

D. Concert A♭ (Your F) Scale with Thirds - Version C

E. Lip Slur #6

F. Five-Step Scale Study - Tongue Two, Slur Two

G. Concert B♭ (Your G) Chord Progression

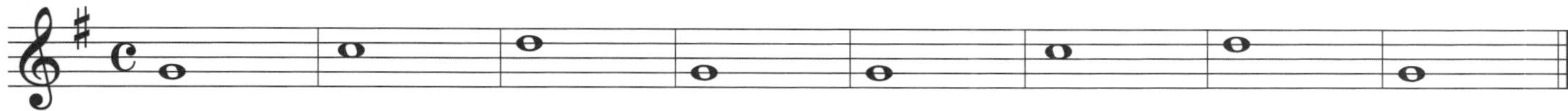

180. When the Saints

Spiritual

A **SIXTEENTH NOTE** receives a quarter of a beat if there is a 4 on the bottom of the time signature; four sixteenth notes fit into one beat.

181. Rhythm Chart

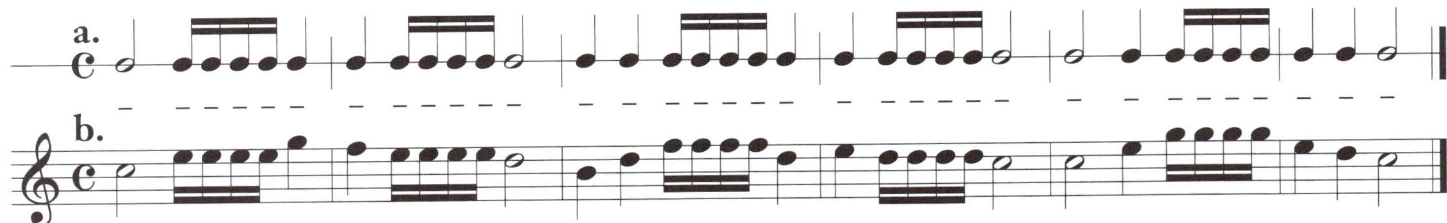

182. The Traveler

183. Hunting Chorus

C. M. von Weber

184. Eine Kleine Nacht Musik

W. A. Mozart

185. The Galway Piper - Playing Test #21

Two sixteenth notes equal an eighth note and an **EIGHTH AND TWO SIXTEENTHS** fit into one beat.

186. Rhythm Study

187. Old Scottish Folk Song

188. William Rides Again

G. Rossini

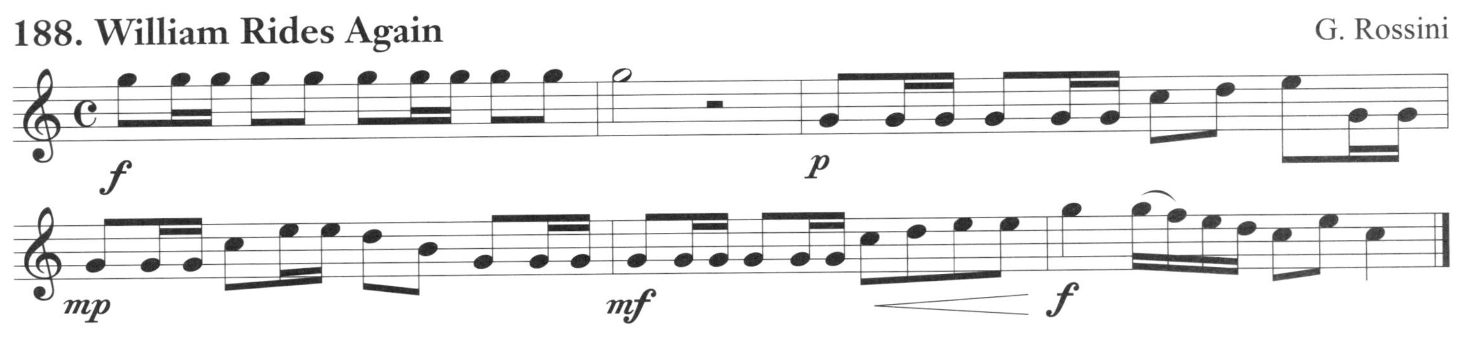

189. Complicated Gifts

Shaker Melody

190. Moroccan Folk Song

191. American Patrol - Playing Test #22

F. W. Meacham

192. Scale, Arpeggio, Thirds, and Chromatic Scale in Concert B♭ (Your G)

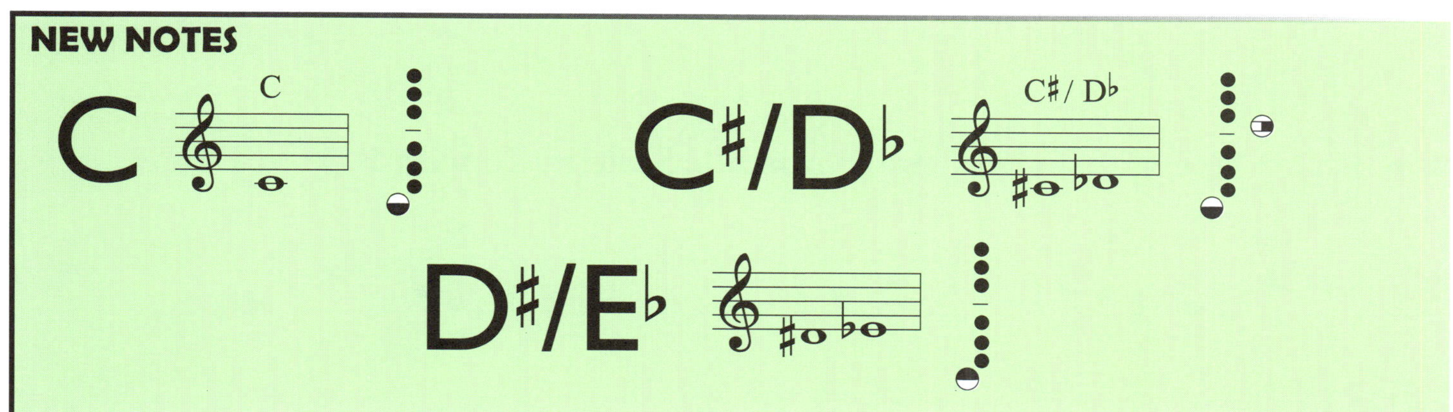

193. Scale, Arpeggio, Thirds, and Chromatic Scale in Concert E♭ (Your C)

194. Scale, Arpeggio, Thirds, and Chromatic Scale in Concert A♭ (Your F)

195. Scale, Arpeggio, Thirds, and Chromatic Scale in Concert C (Your A)

196. Scale, Arpeggio, Thirds, and Chromatic Scale in Concert F (Your D)

197. Scale, Arpeggio, Thirds, and Chromatic Scale in Concert G (Your E)

Supplemental Page

Warm-up Drills

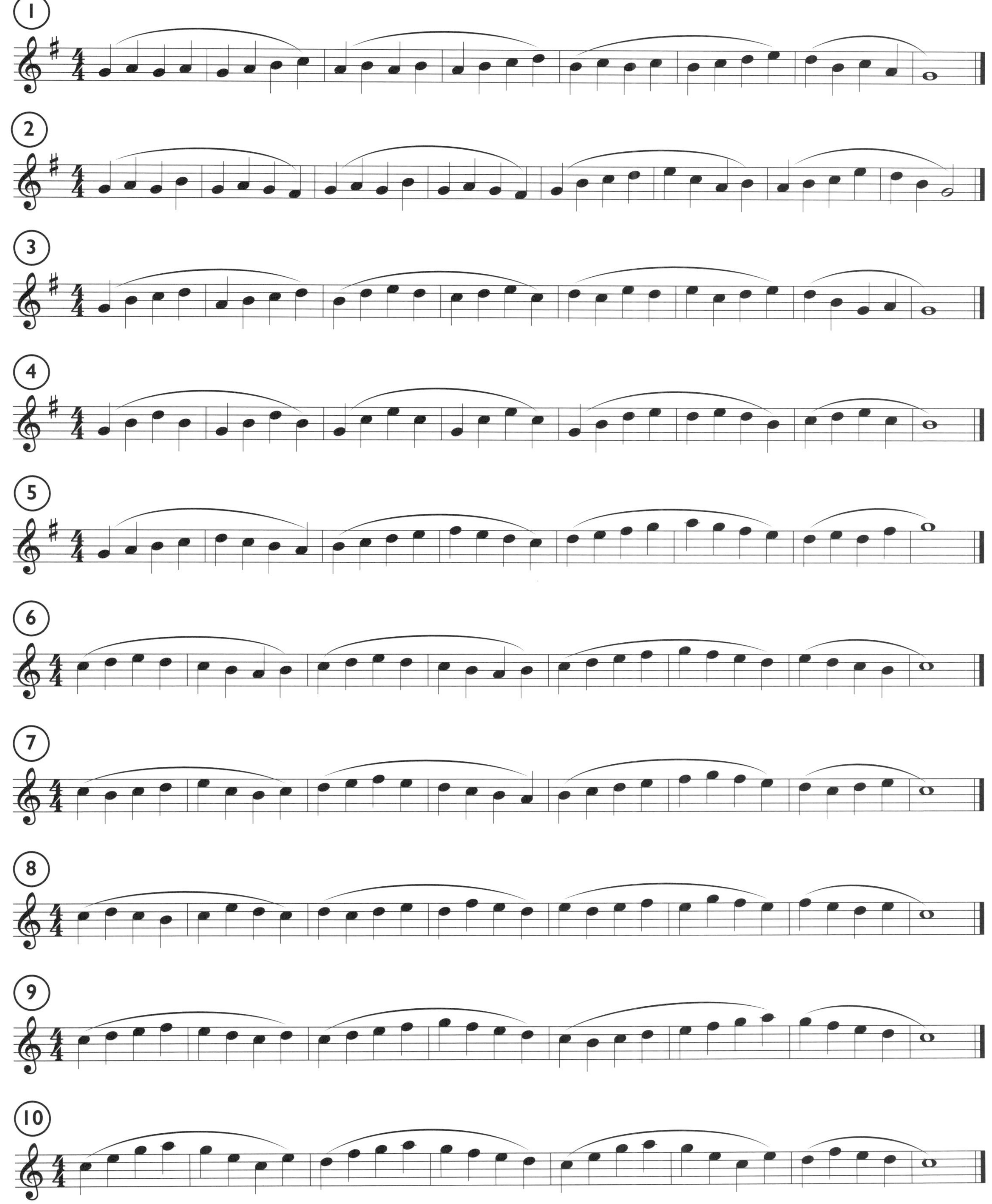

Saxophone Fingering Chart

○ = Open ● = Pressed down